THE MEDICAL USES OF GARLIC

This book is dedicated to the love of Garlic.

Library of Congress Catalog Card Number: 92-83988

Manufactured in the United States of America.

For information write:
GN Communications (Publishing) Ltd.
2600 West Peterson Ave
Chicago, Illinois 60659

Art Direction/Electronic Publishing: Sean Firmiss
Cover Design/Illustrations: Kelly Rauch

Acknowledgments

We wish to thank Vanette Polydoris whose travels to the Far East enhanced our history and knowledge of garlic. We, of course, also thank our respective spouses, Nancy Green and Gloria Polydoris whose support we could not have done without.

Table of Contents

Foreword

The love/hate relationship associated with garlic has always fascinated me. It is used in our food to enhance flavor, in classic literature and modern media it wards off vampires (and friends as well, if you eat too much). Yet, there has been a certain stigma attached to garlic, as if the plant itself must be kept hidden from view. Only recently has the American culture begun to embrace this truly miraculous herb.

My interest in garlic goes back to sometime in my early years in the 1930s at Lincoln School in Evanston, Ill. I had been brought up in two different worlds, which allowed me to experience the values and beliefs of both the Protestant and Greek traditions. I attended a Methodist church and occasionally a Greek Orthodox church. I do speak Greek, although not very well. Consequently, I lived in a very conservative Protestant world on one hand and a very ancient Greek world, with all its customs and belief systems, on the other.

In my home, garlic was served daily. I had it with toast before I went to school to ward off colds and disease during the cold winter months. My dear mother, bless her soul, never learned how to read or write English or Greek, but she knew all about garlic and herbal medicine from traditions passed on to her by previous generations. She never read any of the literature about garlic, be it positive or negative; yet, when our neighbor, Professor Nimms of Northwestern University, would come over she made sure she took garlic off the kitchen table to hide it from him. She knew, somehow, that garlic should not be seen in the kitchen—although she didn't know why.

A very beautiful girl once told me that I smelled because I ate too much garlic. When I was a teenager I overheard two old men (at least my 13-year-old mind thought they were old) talking in Greek. One of the men said he had been eating a lot of garlic, to which the other replied, "You must have a young girlfriend." Somehow, my idea of garlic changed at that point. There must have been something good about it, if this "old" man had a young girlfriend.

Since then, garlic has become somewhat of a minor obsession throughout my travels. Whether I was in Mexico talking to an Indian about Ajo, looking for places where garlic was sold in China, Taiwan, India, Morocco, or casually asking people on trains or planes what they thought of it or whether they took any, this herb has been a constant in my life.

In our own work researching this book, we have found that there has been a tremendous amount of literature and research on the subject of garlic. The explosion of information that has come out within the past five years is unbelievable. In California, many people are experimenting with garlic and garlic oil. The Japanese have begun marketing odorless garlic and are selling it as a panacea. Yet, somehow, in this country the prejudice against garlic, or perhaps more correctly, against its odor, still exists. I hope this book will "peel" away at that prejudice and allow readers to open up to the idea of garlic as a curative herb.

My own suggestions regarding garlic and cancer are offered as a different way of looking at what seems to be an unsolvable problem. As an undergraduate in electrical engineering at Northwestern University, I learned that if you take all the variables of an equation (problem) and lay them out to infinity, you will come out with a very simple answer. (For those of you who don't know what I'm talking about, I am sure some engineer would love to bore you with infinite calculus.) Simply put, with all the variables that exist, the problem to come is insurmountable. Therefore, just take everything to infinity and end up with something plain and simple. In the case of cancer, it does becomes very simple. Just take a little garlic. If you get sick, cut down a little bit. For too long, we have left the cure of cancer in the hands of the medical profession. Unfortunately, they have produced few results so far.

We should no longer have to wait for laboratory research or medical researchers to save our lives. We are 600 years behind in the use of garlic. Perhaps it is time to go back to the wise traditions of our mothers, grandmothers, great grandmothers, and those before them. Maybe the first step is the use of fresh garlic.

There is evidence that chemotherapy works better when accompanied with the process of taking garlic. This has been proven in case studies with laboratory rats and in real life with humans. Is it the odor of garlic? Does the garlic permeate the cancer cells? We don't know yet. And so, we're looking for information. If you are a victim of cancer, perhaps you'll consider this possible treatment. Start with a quarter of a clove a day, and very slowly work up to three or four cloves a day. Garlic seems to work best when it is put through a garlic press. Squashed, pushed, or mashed is how the magic of garlic works. Probably the easiest way to eat garlic is to take a clove of pressed garlic and spread it on toast. My hope is that those who have cancer will try taking garlic in addition to regular medical treatment.

Then, please, take the time to let us know of your experience by sending back the questionnaire at the end of this book. If you try this treatment and the garlic does have an effect, let us know. If nothing happens, let us know that, too. Perhaps it is time we heal ourselves.

You will realize that this work is not an enthusiastic testimonial to garlic from a garlic lover, but a documented study based on a surprising volume of material from clinical studies and research from many continents. It could very well be said that the nutritious and therapeutic value of garlic is proved not only by the experts' findings, which validate those who have used garlic for thousands of years, but also by the undocumented cases, where the use of garlic has led to longer, healthier lives.

Nicholas G. Polydoris

Introduction

For over a decade now, I have been playing in a tennis group with an energetic man of Greek descent who regularly lectures his aging colleagues on the virtues and health values of olive oil and fresh garlic. As an academic physician, I joined my tennis friends in humoring Nick and treating his assertions with considerable skepticism. There was one point in his claims, however, which intrigued me. I had been doing some clinical research on cholesterol in children (diabetic children as well as those with elevated cholesterol levels) and my laboratory had been certified as accurate by the Center for Disease Control. In association with an internationally known colleague, I had become interested in investigating the effects of modern drug therapy on a nine-year-old boy with multiple skin xanthoma and a markedly elevated serum cholesterol. He and his mother had immigrated from Crete several years earlier, and she spoke no English, but she was aware of the high risk these abnormalities could cause her son. After several weeks of study in our Clinical Research Center, there was no change in his condition despite modern drug therapy for these problems. She subsequently returned to Crete with her son.

They returned to the United States one year later and came to see us. There no longer were any skin xanthoma; the cholesterol level, although still mildly elevated, had been markedly reduced. This astonishing occurrence led us to seek what medicines had achieved this miracle. The mother informed us that the child's grandfather in Crete had prescribed daily doses of olive oil throughout the year. Lack of data and the skepticism of editors of medical journals prevented publication of this information, but it was no surprise to Nick that olive oil may have been the curative factor.

Eleven years later, *The New England Journal of Medicine* published a study from The University of Texas Health Science Center entitled "Comparison of mono-unsaturated fatty acids and carbohydrates for lowering plasma cholesterol" (*New Eng. J. Med.* 1986; 314:745-748, March 20). The author, S.M.Grundy, M.D., Ph.D, noted that "in countries such as Greece and in southern Italy, the traditional diet is high in olive oil, and total intake of fat can be high. In these countries, however, both the levels of plasma cholesterol and the rates of coronary heart disease are relatively low." He pointed out that olive oil is rich in oleic acid, a mono-unsaturated fat. Eleven men had entered into a controlled study utilizing a mono-unsaturated fat diet versus two other diets designed to lower cholesterol. On the mono-unsaturated diet, Dr. Grundy found, in these men, a lowering of cholesterol by 13 percent and a lowering of low-density lipoprotein cholesterol (the "bad" kind) by 21 percent. This also was no surprise to Nick.

Recently, when Nick showed me a report in the daily newspaper about a meeting in Washington, D.C., sponsored in part by the Pennsylvania State University, the U.S. Department of Agriculture and an independent nutrition company dedicated to reporting the health aspects of garlic, my academic skepticism was aroused. I knew his testimonials about olive oil had been proven; could it be possible his Greek folklore about garlic would be shown to have some scientific basis also? I went to my computer and modem and entered "PaperChase," the MEDLINE database for references to over 4,000 international scientific journals, available through Beth Israel Hospital. Upon discovering articles in *Nature, Scientific American, Science, Journal of the National Cancer Institute, Cancer Research*, and the many others from prestigious journals listed in the bibliography of this book, I agreed to review this topic for Nick, who was anxious to publish a monograph on the benefits of garlic.

Our unsubstantiated testimonial from the mother of the boy from Crete had been proven correct; perhaps this garlic folklore might have some truth to it also. At any rate, since I was preparing a lecture for medical students on the plant origins of much of our modern medical therapeutic armamentarium, I thought a little Greek mythology might make an intriguing addition. This non-academic, but perhaps interesting, booklet is the product of our combined efforts.

Orville C. Green, III, M.D.

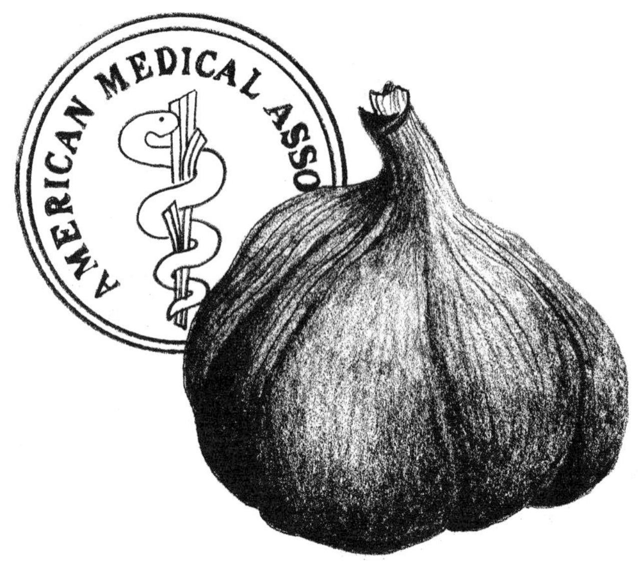

Prologue

This book has been prepared by two voices: one, a trained professional in the field of academic medicine, and the other, an expert in the history and uses of garlic in folklore and modern society. We have collected information that is documented in authoritative scientific journals and have attempted to relate this information to traditional ethnic uses of garlic as herbal medicine. Our purpose is to provide this knowledge in terms that are understandable to the average person without special training or background in this field.

We believe that garlic has beneficial qualities that have been well known and useful to all societies from the primitive to the modern but that these qualities have been ignored by medical practitioners for a variety of social reasons. Now, in the past few years, scientists have become increasingly aware of the many folklore reports of cures and improvements in the health of patients with infections, heart disease, immune disorders, lipid (cholesterol and fat) disorders, and recently, tumors and cancers.

These facts have led university researchers, commercial drug houses and the National Institute of Health to devote large sums of money in support of research into the natural products found in plants, including garlic. It will be many years before the findings benefit humanity. Meanwhile, this book will provide information about the therapeutic uses of garlic. The information is based upon ancient folklore knowledge as well as upon recent scientific findings.

We have tried in this book to enumerate facts that will withstand the scrutiny of skeptical medical professionals. At the same time, we hope to explain how these facts may be of help to individuals. In proper moderation, garlic may be useful without altering standard medical programs or endangering an individual's health. The information outlined here comes from research sources and medical journals with prestigious reputations and accepted critical review procedures.

References are listed at the end of this book. The reader interested in substantiation of the scientific evidence referred to in the discussions is directed to these references for detailed methodology and descriptions of the experiments. We predict

that the underlying chemical compounds found in the fresh herbal preparations of garlic will ultimately prove to be as beneficial to humanity as have the many medicinal preparations (reviewed below) now in daily use in standard medical practices. These uses owe their discovery to folklore knowledge of healing plants in primitive as well as modern societies.

History and Lore

For most of mankind's history, shamans, medicine men and physicians were forced to rely upon natural substances in the search for therapeutic remedies other than faith healing. Over the centuries, many plants were found to be useful by utilizing their leaves, seeds or bark in a carefully calculated dose and in a variety of fashions, often compounded in secret mixtures. The basic ingredients in these plant preparations responsible for successful treatments remained obscure until adequate methods for separation of chemical compounds could be developed.

During the 19th century, German chemists revolutionized organic chemistry with new techniques of synthesis of a wide variety of compounds useful in industry and medicine. For medicinal agents being sought from nature, the approach taken initially in these laboratories was to attempt isolation of the active principle, then identify its structure and synthesize it in pure form. As a result of these analytic and synthetic techniques, major discoveries of medicine resulted from investigations into folklore remedies; a partial list of important medications in use today includes opiates, quinine, digitalis, quinidine, ouabain, squill, aspirin, vitamins, reserpine, colchicine, cocaine, laxatives (bran, agar, tragacanth, gums), cathartics (castor oil, senna, cascara sagrada, aloe, danthron), psoralens, anti-cancer drugs (vincristine, vinblastine), and taxol (from the bark of the Pacific eucalyptus tree, effective in treating ovarian cancer and other cancers). For a detailed review of plant sources for these medications, see the Appendix.

How do plant products act in human tissues? Recent investigations have revealed that there are tissue "receptors" in human tissues for compounds made in plants. Receptors are the proteins within cells that attract and bind specific compounds; these compounds may arrive at the cell through circulation in the blood stream, or through neighboring cells. The binding of drugs to receptors is the accepted theory of activity even though research efforts still must discover the specific intracellular receptors for most drugs and how they act after the binding occurs.

One of the fascinating speculations resulting from this concept of receptor requirement for drug

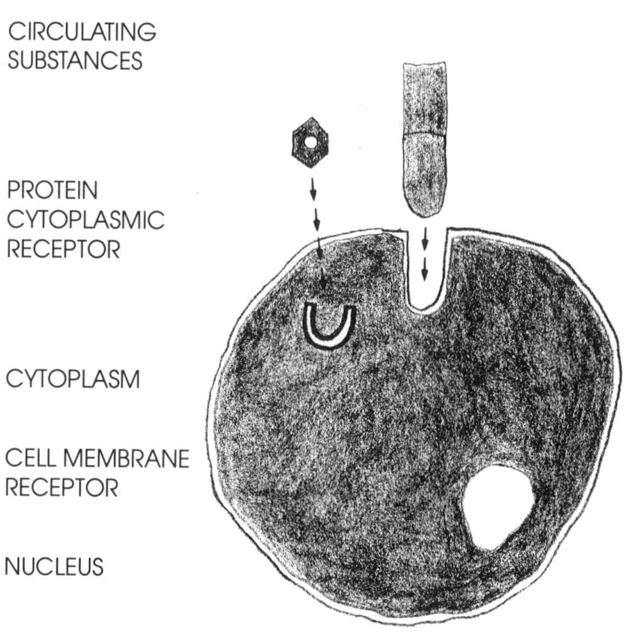

Reaction of Plant Products In Human Tissue

There are two major types of receptors, each for specific substances. One type is part of the cell membrane; the other type is within the cell cytoplasm, usually a protein. The combination of a circulating substance with its specific receptor initiates specific reactions within the cell.

activity in human cells is how it proves an evolutionary relationship of all cellular life, whether it be plant or animal. How else can one conceive of our brain, heart, bowel, or any human tissue, containing specific receptors for compounds made by plants for use in their own cells? The discovery of human brain cell receptors for morphine, for example, has led to an explosion of knowledge (and a Nobel prize) of how the human brain works to control pain impulses and emotions (endorphins, enkephalins, etc.). Receptors for a single compound may often be found in multiple body tissues and organs and therefore response to a drug may be manifest in multiple sites. Thus, plant-derived drugs may have multiple effects in humans: i.e. opiates affect the brain, the cough reflex, and the bowel (constipation).

Almost all the useful compounds isolated from plants were found to have multiple effects in the human body. When the desired effect was accompanied by effects on other tissues and organs, these additional effects were termed "side effects." At high enough dosage levels, they became "toxic side effects," a property of almost all drugs available today whether or not of plant origin. A vast business grew out of the desire to attempt modification of these natural compounds in modern laboratories in the effort to seek a new derivative compound that would exert the desired effect but be dissociated from the so-called "side effects."

At present, large numbers of drugs are prepared in the laboratories of the major marketing drug houses, utilizing as starting substrates these natural sources of proven therapeutic efficacy, in attempts to synthesize "new" compounds that are delivered to physicians after prolonged clinical testing. Unfortunately, all these variations upon natural sources continue to have multiple side effects in the human body, sometimes with results that are devastatingly worse than the original natural leaf, seed or bark that achieved initial fame with folklore healers. (To the dismay of the medical profession, such disasters have provided fertile fields for maintaining the wealth of the legal profession.)

The reason for these difficulties often lies in a basic therapeutic principle: a useful drug must have a desired therapeutic effect that provides a margin of safety before the dosage level reaches a toxic or other undesirable effect; the corollary to this principle is that whenever the potency is increased, (i.e., the number of milligrams required for therapy is decreased by chemical manipulation), then the margin of safety per milligram dose is also reduced, and in some potent drugs, the margin of safety has essentially disappeared.

Thus the various chemical alterations of these basic compounds are frequently accompanied by alterations in margins of safety for the many side effects, and new side effects may also appear. It is not surprising that natural compounds that evolved in living cells, whether they be plant or animal, have gone through many years of natural selection to achieve a reasonable margin of safety and that the original form of the therapeutic agent as found in plant life may be the safest.

Alternatively, some plants have developed, for defensive reasons, compounds that are extremely toxic when the entire plant is eaten but may have some human therapeutic usefulness when used in very small quantities. These plants have also given us valuable medications—antimicrobials, anti-helminthics, paralytics (curare derivatives), antimuscarinics (scopolamine, atropine, belladonna), strychnine, picrotoxin, ergot and others.

Laboratory scientists working in this field of drug synthesis and experimentation are basically competing with "Mother Nature;" they have developed an artificial model of evolution of new compounds by chemical means rather than by mutation and natural selection. Unfortunately, the time period of "testing" these new drugs in a few years or less has been so greatly reduced over the millennia of natural evolution that a true evaluation of safety of many of these new drugs cannot be achieved.

Today, we are best advised to recognize that all exogenous drugs, whether they be in their natural form or chemically modified, when given to humans will have multiple effects on a variety of organ systems. Therefore, all drugs will have a toxic potential at some dose level, which may vary widely in different individuals with different rates of absorption, metabolism, degradation and excretion. This holds true for natural compounds found in plants and animals as well, and the study of these variables is the basis for the science of pharmacology.

Therefore, in the discussions that follow, it must be kept in mind that ingestion of plant (and animal) products with known or speculative therapeutic potential can have toxic as well as beneficial effects if precautions to maintain a margin of safety in dosage are ignored. The ancient shamans knew this, and kept their formulations as well-guarded secrets to be passed on only to apprentices.

In an effort to increase present day knowledge of folklore secrets, a group of scientists called "ethnobotanists" are now active in research. These scientists combine anthropology and botany in efforts to learn the secrets of shamans whose knowledge resulted from thousands of years of trial and error using plants for therapy.

Dr. Michael Balick, director of the Institute of Economic Botany of the New York Botanical Garden, is one of these scientists. He says "of more than 265,000 known plant species, less than 1% have been tested for medical applications or even for the chemical compounds they contain....yet out of this tiny portion have come 25 percent of medicines" (Goleman 1991). Balick, along with several colleagues, is supported by a $2.5 million contract from the National Cancer Institute to conduct research into ethnobotany and collect plants that may be useful in therapy of cancer and other diseases. One source of his research is the shamanic knowledge of primitive tribes in rain forests and other isolated areas. Eli Lilly and Co. has made an investment of $4 million in a California company, Shaman Pharmaceuticals, Inc., which employs ethnobotanists to work with rain forest shamans to seek the folklore plants and phytochemicals used by these tribal medicine men; these plants are then brought to the laboratories of the company for further studies.

As a result of these new studies in many laboratories, scientists have now aroused increasing interest in garlic as a medicinal. This interest stems from the use of garlic in many ethnic communities today; the anecdotal results are now withstanding detailed statistical proof of efficacy. These scientific studies and the folklore anecdotes are reviewed in the chapters that follow.

Garlic as a Medicinal

History

While in modern times we have primarily used garlic as a spice, our ancestors had a great respect for the herb as much more than a flavor-enhancer. From the Egyptians to the Indians to the Chinese, garlic has been part of the diet of the Eastern world for centuries. Garlic (and onion) was often referred to as medication in the most ancient of writings. Dr. Eric Block, Professor of Chemistry at the State University of New York in Albany, has reviewed some of this history (Block 1985).

An Egyptian papyrus, the Ebers Codex of about 1500 B.C., mentions garlic as therapy for many illnesses including tumors, worms, arthritis, and heart disorders. Cheops, first king of the IV Dynasty of Egypt, used to inform his people of the virtues of garlic. The builders of the Great Pyramids were said to have fed garlic to the slaves to strengthen them for the task in 3000 B.C. The Egyptian tomb of King Tut is reported to have contained several garlic bulbs along with the other treasures. Hippocrates, the "Father of Medicine" (4th century B.C.) mentions garlic as a medicinal and wrote "your food must be medicine—and your medicine must be food." Pliny the Elder (1st century A.D.—died in 79 A.D. while trying to observe closely an eruption of Vesuvius) mentions therapeutic uses of garlic and onions in his only surviving work, "Historia Naturalis." In ancient Greece, athletes of the Olympic games would chew garlic before competing in the belief it gave them strength. Galinos and Discouridis, great physicians of ancient Greece, described garlic as a diuretic and a medicine against tapeworm, asthma, jaundice, tooth pain and even acne. The herb was also used as an antidote for poison. Garlic was prescribed as a vermifuge for the Roman army in the first century A.D. and the soldiers also believed it gave them superior strength to perform heroic deeds.

Garlic has a long tradition in India and Russia as an antiseptic for wounds and is reported to have been used as recently as World War II. A garlic potion called "vinaigre des quatre voleurs" is still in use in France as a preventive for disease, having become famous during the plague of 1721, when it was said to have given immunity to certain gravediggers (who were four thieves—"quatre voleurs"—condemned to that task).

Our Colonial forefathers are reported to have wrapped garlic cloves around the feet and placed garlic in the shoes of smallpox victims, thus recording what may be the oldest form of transdermal therapy. In 1858, Louis Pasteur reported garlic to have antibacterial effects. Albert Schweitzer is said to have used it for amoebic dysentery in Africa.

Why have these leads not been followed up by past medical practitioners? Why has garlic not received the same attention given to other folklore and shamanic cures? It is possible that modern society has shunned this history of therapeutic effectiveness because of the odor associated with ingestion of fresh garlic.

Until recently, the medicinal uses of garlic seemed to have been divided between rich and poor, high and low social classes, modern cultures and those rich with history and traditions. An interesting example is the story of English soldiers of World War II stationed at Gibraltar, where garlic is worshipped with a passion. Uncharacteristically, these soldiers avoided the local Spanish girls, not for fear of disease, but because the soldiers could not stand the garlic smell. English officers inviting Gibraltans to play cards told their guests that they could not bring their cloves of garlic with them, which they were accustomed to consuming along with soft drinks at such games. (This story seems to confirm the Anglo-American aversion to strong odors, but the aversion appears to be selective for odors generated by individuals; the odors of noxious industrial fumes, smogs, burning fuels and tobacco seem ignored.)

Often, Sicilians visiting America brought with them whole tresses of garlic as a gift to their relatives. They believed garlic could not be grown in America. The seizure by Customs Officers of these imported products caused strong protests; it seems that the uninformed customs authorities considered garlic as a Mafia weapon and a source of fear.

These aversions to garlic consumption and the associated odors continue in several cultures including our own. It is our contention that the benefits may outweigh the artificial and unnatural social fixation upon the need for the human body to have no odor.

Folklore

> "Eat a piece of garlic to maintain your health and put one in your pocket to keep away the evil eye."

This was one of the sayings of Nick's grandmother. Annette Polydoris lived to be 105 years old and could relate many legends of Greek folklore herbal medicine she had learned as a child. It was a strange mixture of herbs, lotions, witchcraft and magic potions. But through all the mythic tales there was the recurrent theme of garlic. The "evil eye" was a constant threat to human beings, especially to newly born infants, and midwives required that garlic be present as a protection at birth. Garlic bulbs placed over the doorways of homes also protect against evil and it is said that bunches of garlic over their doorways will protect Greek women against the jealous Nereids (beautiful nymphs, or mermaids) who will steal their husbands. Greek businessmen can occasionally be found to have a small bit of garlic in their wallets to assure success in their transactions.

As far back as the Homeric legend of Odysseus, garlic has had magic powers. In the translation by T. E. Shaw the god Hermes gave Odysseus a potent herb called "Moly," which protected him against the poisonous drugs of Circe, who had turned his men into swine; Moly is thought to be one of the forms of garlic.

In Korean culture, garlic is also highly esteemed. According to one Korean legend, the king of the heavens had a son named Hwnwoong who was interested in human activity. So the king allowed his son to come down to earth and he gave him 3,000 soldiers plus the staff for controlling wind, rain and clouds. One day, so the legend says, a tiger and a bear, both females who lived together in a cave, came to Hwnwoong pleading to be changed into human beings. Hwnwoong gave each of them 20 pieces of garlic and one bundle of mug plant and told them to stay in the cave without sunlight for 100 days. The tiger could not obey this order but the bear did, and so after 100 days turned into a lady. But she was lonely and prayed to Hwnwoong because she wanted to have a baby. Hwnwoong answered her prayers by transforming himself into a

human being and marrying her. The two had a son who became the first king of ancient Korea.

Myths such as these reflect ways of thinking of human origins. But why did Hwnwoong choose garlic and mud plant? Koreans, as well as other cultures, believed garlic had mysterious and powerful functions. And, of course, there is the well known use of garlic to protect against vampires, a theme commonly used in movies and horror stories today. There are some tales that defy belief, such as the one that claims Eric the 4th of France chewed garlic before attempting a new love affair; there are those in France who claim that the famous Three Musketeers were so good at fighting off the enemy because of all the garlic they consumed—perhaps more believable but a myth nonetheless.

Those are some of the myths that are interesting tales but are without substantial supporting evidence. If you listen to people from the Mediterranean area, there are many variations of garlic and olive oil taken together and separately for health reasons, during periods of famine and disease and in many cases simply for prevention of disease. In the cultural traditions of the Greek Orthodox church today, it is still a common practice to consume fish and skordalia after visiting a funeral home to pay respects to a dead person: the fish as a Christian symbol and the fresh garlic preparation, skordalia, as a preventive against possible transmission of the disease that caused the death. These stories come from other parts of the world also; wherever garlic and onions are grown stories are found about their medicinal values.

Today, the Japanese are one of the best customers of commercial garlic preparations (the odorless forms), and folklore stories of its medicinal value have been passed on for generations in Oriental cultures. In Korea, a garlic preparation, Kim Chee, is both a health food and a medication. In Russia, there is a saying: "Eat leeks in March and garlic in May, and the rest of the year, your physician may play."

Modern Investigations

Chemists in several university laboratories have become interested in searching for the specific chemicals in garlic and onions that may be responsible for the various effects of these plants. Today, more than one hundred compounds have been identified and many more are being investigated. The first chemist to obtain compounds from garlic was Wertheim (one of the previously mentioned German researchers), who recognized in 1844 that the sulfur components were responsible for the flavor and odor and that the compounds had a chemical structure involving two terminal carbon atoms separated by a double bond (C3H5). He named these chemical structures "allyl" compounds, after the botanical name for garlic, "Allium sativum." (The generic name "Allium" refers to many plants of the lily family.) Wertheim's assignment of the name "allyl" has persisted in the organic chemistry literature for compounds with a chemical structure similar to those he found. Later, other German chemists identified additional compounds with larger chemical structures, (diallyl disulfide, diallyl trisulfide and diallyl tetrasulfide). Onions were found to have different chemical structures, but these also contained sulfur.

There seems to have been little interest in these compounds until 1944 when chemists at the Sterling-Winthrop Chemical Company isolated the oxide of diallyl disulfide and gave it the name "Allicin" (Cavallito 1944). They found it to be the liquid that is responsible for the garlic odor, but also discovered that it was capable of killing a variety of bacteria and fungi in very dilute solutions. Later, in 1948, chemists at the Sandoz Company in Basel, Switzerland, discovered why garlic bulbs have no odor until cut or ground up: allicin is not formed in the garlic clove until an enzyme in the cells activates a precursor compound, which is then enzymatically converted to allicin. They named the enzyme "allinase" and the precursor compound "alliin." Purification of alliin revealed it to be odorless (Stoll 1951).

More recently, these compounds have been investigated for their medicinal properties. Studies by Dr. Block, in association with investigators worldwide, resulted in the isolation and characterization of a derivative compound, which he named "ajoene" (the Spanish word for garlic is"ajo") (Block 1984). This compound has been found to prevent clotting of blood in humans by inhibiting platelet aggregation (a process in which small components in the blood aggregate, or stick together, and start the formation of clots), and this effect is as potent as aspirin, which has now been demonstrated through clinical research studies to be an effective agent in preventing heart attacks.

As mentioned earlier, Louis Pasteur found that garlic contained antibacterial qualities. This effect was further studied and confirmed by chemists Cavallito and Bailey in 1944. In a second study, Cavallito and co-authors described the chemical structure of allicin, which was the effective agent (Cavallito, Buck, Suter 1944). In addition, studies at the School of Medicine of the University of Medicine and Dentistry in Newark, New Jersey, have shown that a fresh extract of garlic given by mouth to human volunteers resulted in antifungal activity in the serum but the effect was transient (Caporaso 1983).

Of interest, there was no effect with the commercial oral capsules, again demonstrating the requirement that garlic must be fresh for therapeutic effect. This antifungal effect in the serum of volunteers was not considered potent enough to replace present commercial antifungal drugs at this time but was adequate to confirm folklore reports of its use for this purpose.

Because of the antibacterial and antifungal effects mentioned above, Dr. Block has proposed that allicin is present in garlic as an evolutionary protection against bulb decay by fungi and bacteria. Allicin is present in almost all garlic preparations as well as the fresh cut or ground bulb. Ajoene is found only in fresh garlic and Dr. Block has not found it to be present in the various powders, pills, oils and extracts available on the market today. Shamanic treatments have always required fresh, not cooked, garlic.

As noted earlier, Dr. Block has isolated a potent compound ajoene from garlic, which has a significant antithrombotic effect in the clotting of blood due to platelet aggregation. Ajoene is found only in fresh garlic. This antithrombotic effect has also been noted in experimental animals with constricted coronary arteries, preventing clot formation secondary to platelet aggregation (DeBoer 1989). The aggregation of platelets is considered to be one major cause of heart attacks (coronary thrombosis).

Garlic and its products have been reported to have beneficial effects upon atherosclerosis and lipid metabolism with a lowering of cholesterol and triglyceride levels. The decline in serum triglyceride levels may be secondary to inhibition of fat digestion (Gargouri 1989). A review of the medical literature on this subject has been published in the medical journal, *Nutrition Research* (Lau 1983) and an international symposium on the cardiovascular effects of garlic, investigating the chemistry, pharmacology and medical applications in humans was held in Germany in 1989 (*Cardiol Pract* volume 10, Supplement, pages 1-15). The evidence for the beneficial effects in humans is supported by these European reports although a thorough clinical study has not been undertaken and the mechanism is unclear.

A report from India indicated that men surviving a first heart attack and eating up to four cloves of garlic a day (six to ten grams) were protected against a second heart attack as compared with men who did not eat garlic (Goldfinger 1991). Results in both rodents and human beings have shown promising effects, indicating the need for further research in this important area.

For centuries, garlic has been used as a folklore medicine for diabetes in Asia, Europe and the Middle East and is one of the effective plant medicines for that disease (Bailey 1989). Recent research studies show that minced garlic induced a lowering of blood sugar (hypoglycemia) as a result of stimulation of insulin secretion in rodents in several experimental laboratories including that of the U.S. Department of Agriculture in Maryland (Chang and Johnson 1980) and the Department of Chemistry at the University of Delaware (Jain 1973, 1975). Results in human beings have not been established by definitive laboratory methods using insulin assays but reports from India provide some evidence of a hypoglycemic effect in humans also. The possibility that garlic or extracts contain a substance that can stimulate insulin secretion in humans should be investigated further since present medications for this purpose often have undesirable side effects.

There is a report in *Federation Proceedings* (Kandil, et al 1987) where human volunteers ate 0.5 grams of raw garlic daily for three weeks. Blood samples were taken to test effectiveness of one type of their white blood cells against cultured tumor cells in laboratory bottles. The white blood cells that were studied were those called "Killer Cells." Those who took the garlic had blood cells that were more effective killers of tumor cells than control blood samples from individuals who did not take garlic. The difference was found to be effective but of minimal statistical significance, however, and this abstract has not yet been published in detail to allow critical evaluation of the methodology.

An earlier report in *Nature* demonstrated that if tumor cells were pretreated with an extract of garlic and then injected into mice, the mice demonstrated a strong immunity to the subsequent injection of untreated cells of the same tumor, whereas untreated cells injected alone into mice resulted in no immunity to the tumor. (Fujiwara 1967). These two studies appear to have more relevance to tumor therapy than to responses to other immunologic stimuli such as bacteria and viruses.

Cancer — Studies and Results

Garlic—its oil and extracts—has been studied extensively in animal research. The results have demonstrated that garlic inhibits the growth of a variety of cancers and tumors. Early reports on the effect of garlic therapy for tumors did not appear promising (DiPaolo 1960), but more recent reports with garlic extracts have led cancer researchers to investigate garlic and its compounds in more detail. Most of these studies have been carried out in rodents (mice, rats, hamsters, rabbits) but results in India, China, Italy and Hawaii have indicated that garlic preparations have anti-carcinogenic effects in humans also.

A review of the relationship of garlic to malignant disease was published in 1990 (Dausch 1990) and a summary of recent results was recently presented at a scientific conference in Washington, D.C., held in August, 1990, and reported in the news media.

Dr. John A. Milner of the Nutrition department at Penn State found that garlic inhibits by 70 percent the development of breast cancer in laboratory rats, confirming earlier reports in mice (Kroening 1964). Garlic also inhibits the carcinogenic action of aflotoxins, which occur naturally in peanuts and corn. Studies in animals at the M.D. Anderson Cancer Center in Houston and also at Pennsylvania State University have shown that garlic compounds can interfere with the action of other carcinogens that cause cancer of the colon, rectum, and esophagus. These reports and a summary of the conference were reported in *Science and Health* (Martin 1990).

In China, there has been a centuries-long tradition of using garlic to treat tumors and malignancies. Dr. William J. Blot of the National Cancer Institute reported on previously published studies in China and Italy showing that eaters of garlic, onions, and scallions had much lower rates of stomach cancer than those who did not eat these plants (You and Blot, et al 1989). The reasons are speculative at present but possibilities include the potent effect of garlic products in acting to block the formation of carcinogenic nitrosamines (compounds found in cured meats and foods which have been cooked over charcoal or charred directly) as well as the possibility that the bactericidal effect of allicin may suppress the growth of certain bacteria (Helicobacter pylori) that grow in the stomach in spite of its acid content. This bacterium is now thought to be responsible for stomach inflammation, ulcers, and cancer. Allicin, a proven bactericidal agent, unlike many antibiotics, is not destroyed in an acid environment and can thus act on these bacteria in the stomach.

Other possible causes for the anticarcinogenic effects of garlic, including detoxification, alteration of enzymatic activity and blockage of carcinogens from reaching cellular DNA, have been reviewed in detail and the point is made that sulfur-containing compounds have long been known to be effective in these mechanisms (Dausch 1990). The specific compound, ajoene, kills malignant tumor cells of a type known as Burkitt's lymphoma when added to tissue cultures of those cells (Goldfinger 1991).

Reports have appeared in respected scientific journals on the effectiveness of garlic extracts in the prevention of a variety of experimentally induced cancers in rodents. Some experimenters have used an extract prepared by squeezing peeled fresh garlic; others have used oral dose preparations utilizing the oil from fresh garlic, dissolved in mineral oil in concentrations of 0.5% up to 50 %. These preparations have prevented the development of experimentally induced oral cancer in hamsters and hepatocarcinogenic (liver cancer) responses in rats (Meng 1990).

Induced skin tumors in rodents have been prevented by administration of garlic oil (Perchellett 1985, 1990). At Western Reserve University in New Jersey, a crystalline derivative of an extract from garlic was found to be an effective agent in protecting mice injected with live sarcoma tumor cells if the cells were preincubated in saline with minute quantities of the garlic extract; additionally, if untreated cells were injected into mice who then received an injection of the garlic derivative, tumor growth was inhibited and in some of the mice, completely prevented. (Wiesberger and Pensky 1957, 1958). A chemical named DMBA causes cancer when applied to the skin of mice, and this effect can be inhibited or blocked by treatment with garlic and onion oils (Belman 1983, 1989, 1990).

None of these basic research studies is directly applicable to human beings and there is as yet no published evidence that garlic will cure any cancer; but these investigative leads are promising enough to warrant further research. The data appear to indicate that the anticancer effects of garlic act in a variety of animals (including humans) and upon a variety of tumors. As a result of recent renewed interest in these proven effects of garlic, the National Cancer Institute has begun clinical trials and is supporting investigators with several million dollars in grants to study plant sources of possible anticarcinogens. Interested readers are referred to the list of references at the end of the book.

Recommendations for Use

Garlic preparations for ingestion include the bulb, the cloves which make up the bulb, proprietary pills, garlic powders and the juice and pulp obtained from crushing in a garlic press. Ideally, these preparations should be taken at mealtime with food. The method recommended is to begin with 1/4 clove of garlic with a meal and slowly increase to one or two full cloves. For therapeutic effects, three to four cloves daily would be recommended as a minimum. It has been reported that some older persons eat a whole bulb daily without ill effects (a bulb consists of a number of cloves).

One clove of garlic is thought to be equal to about eight proprietary garlic pills but this is only an approximation since cloves vary in size and pills may vary in size and quantity. Garlic powder tablets are available and depending upon the manufacturer and clove size, one clove will give 300 to 900 milligrams of powder.

Researchers have used a fresh extract of garlic made by homogenizing 100 grams of fresh garlic cloves (about three large bulbs, or forty cloves) in a Waring blendor in the cold followed by centrifuging and filtering, using the extract (Caporaso 1983). Of interest, the human volunteer subjects in that study were able to tolerate only 25 ml (less than one ounce—30 ml) of this extract orally before complaining of burning sensations in the esophagus and some vomiting. This represents a very large dosage of garlic when compared with the average clove, which weighs in the range of three grams and produces about 1.5 ml of extract when squeezed in a press.

In May of 1991, British botanist Murat Ozsoy, managing director of Twyford Plant Laboratories in Somerset, England, announced that he had developed a strain of odorless garlic after cross breeding different strains for more than three years. Whether this form of garlic will have the same beneficial effects as the traditional plant is unknown since allicin is the compound responsible for both the odor and the antibacterial activity of garlic.

Garlic lovers report differences in garlic flavors depending upon the source; garlic grown in Crete has a flavor different from garlic grown in California and the "elephant garlic" now appearing in stores is milder and less flavorable. These variations in flavor, and presumably potency, are most likely due to variations in the mineral and other nutrient contents of the soil in which the bulb is grown.

Garlic preparations are commercially available as dried powders, tablets, capsules of garlic oil, and capsules of aged extracts, as well as a variety of other forms. In most of the studies reviewed here, however, the most effective form has been found to be fresh garlic itself.

It is unfortunate that there is no method for determination of the potencies of the various available garlic preparations. A simple labeling of the content of allicin and ajoene for each variety would provide a beginning and allow comparison with fresh garlic cloves. If garlic cloves, or chemical derivatives isolated from the cloves, are to be used in clinical trials or any forms of therapy, some assay procedure must be developed or evaluation of research results among investigators using animals and humans will be difficult. The lack of such studies to provide equivalence between the many preparations available is undoubtedly the cause of some of the skepticism in the medical profession.

There are approximately seven calories per clove. In addition to the beneficial organic compounds, garlic contains small amounts of calcium, selenium, germanium and vitamins, all in insignificant amounts. The fiber content of fresh garlic may be a useful component in view of modern concepts of the beneficial effects of dietary fiber.

Prof sniffs cold cure: garlic

Newhouse News Service

NEW OR
ray is here
grandmoth
helps fight
Murray,
ment wit
research.
The n
Brigham
found th
an all-p
causin
causes
Garl
that c
rator
bacte

Byron Mur-

90 percent of a virus in a laboratory dish within 30 minutes.
To get the best out of garlic,
...ldn't wear it in a bag
... your grand-

EXCITING NEWS FROM THE FIRST WORLD GARLIC CONGRESS

GARLIC: A Clove a Day May Fight Cancer, Heart Disease and Infection

Reports from the First World Congress on the Health Significance of Garlic, held in Washington, D.C.:

➤ A scientis...

Since those are two of the most common reasons the body rejects artificial devices, Dr. Hermes figured that a garlic-based coating could boost the odds that ...

none. And when they cultured rat liver cells in test tubes with the garlic extracts, triglyceride synthesis was reduced by 40 percent and cholesterol production by half.

How much garlic is needed to get that heart-healthy result? Dr. Yeh fed his rats 2 percent of their diets as garlic, which really isn't that much, he says. "It's about five cloves a day, but we have to do more animal studies to find out if this is a safe level. It's possible that a lower intake may still be effective. That's one of the things we have to establish—the safe and effective dose—before we start experimenting in people. But human studies are our ultimate goal."

Herbal arsenal

Garlic and its cousins may be the best weapons yet in preventing disease

By Jeff Lyon

In 1951, before she would become world famous as the prima donna of the Bolshoi Ballet, Galina Vishnevskaya lay in a Russian sanitarium dying of tuberculosis.

A new wonder drug called streptomycin had only just become available in the Soviet Union. At her doctor's insistence, Vishnevskaya submitted to a painful series of 120 shots.

The antibiotic had its effect. But as Vishnevskaya tells it, she did not really begin to get better until she prescribed for herself half a pound a day of a humble herb that has been used as a folk remedy since the time of the pharaohs.

To this day Vishnevskaya, now a celebrated artist who is married to cellist and conductor Mstislav Rostropovich, attributes her survival to the strong-smel-...

At Houston's M.D. Anderson Hospital, cancer researcher Michael Wargowich specializes in chemoprevention—the warding off of malignancies through natural foods and extracts. He has reported startling success in using garlic compounds to prevent cancer of the stomach and esophagus in rats.

"This is no longer nutritional-food-store stuff," Wargowich says. "At our hospital, two cancer research sections, gastrointestinal and head and neck, have committed themselves to chemopreventive studies. We realize that this presents a roadblock to a lot of tumors, and a lot of specialists in early cancers now consider this the way to go. It's really exciting."

The National Cancer Institute has made chemoprevention a priority, seeking hard evidence for the growing suspicion that the produce section at the supermarket is an untapped

... and infections for centuries.

... percent and 15 percent lower, respectively, in rats fed garlic compared to rats who got

... vampires being repelled by garlic don't scare us sophisticated, late-20th-century Westerners, what about a modern bogey-man—cancer? Here, too,

Toxicity or Sensitivity

There is no evidence that ingestion of garlic will interfere with any standard medical therapy for any disorder. As of 1990, there is no report on toxicity in humans from garlic in the files of The National Toxicological Program of the U. S. Government (Dausch 1990). The possibility exists that the antithrombiotic effect of ajoene may cause spontaneous bleeding in persons taking aspirin or other drugs such as warfarin (coumadin) to prevent blood clots but no reports of this problem are known. As mentioned previously, ingestion of garlic juice and pulp from fresh cloves without ingestion of other foods may cause a burning sensation in the mouth or esophagus and even induce vomiting when taken in large quantities. Intolerance to the oral intake of 3.75 milligrams of essential oil of garlic over a period of daily ingestion for 12 weeks has been reported (Arora 1981). In another report, however, human subjects have ingested 15 milligrams of the essential oil daily with minimal side effects (Bordia 1981). As noted earlier, human volunteers in another study could not tolerate more than 10 to 25 cc of garlic juice daily (Caporaso 1983).

Dried garlic pills are well tolerated in a dose of 600 milligrams daily; garlic powder tablets were well tolerated in a dosage of 21 grams daily (equal to 64 grams of fresh garlic); these powders and tablets, however, are not thought to have the full beneficial effects of fresh garlic or its oil. To minimize any problems, it is always recommended that all forms of garlic be eaten with other foods.

There have been several studies on toxicity in animals receiving huge doses of garlic and its products. These include studies where 10 milligrams of garlic oil injected into mice caused death; prolonged feeding of raw garlic caused anemia and poor growth in rats; feeding raw garlic extract to rodents caused a decrease in bowel bacterial count; the LD50 (50 percent live-"L;" 50 percent die-"D") is reported to require a dose greater than 30 ml/Kg body weight in rodents (Dausch 1990). These all are very large doses in small animals and are not relevant to the quantities able to be ingested by humans.

Those individuals with sensitivity to onions may find they are also sensitive to forms of garlic. The most common complaints are abdominal distress, heartburn, and flatulence, but other forms of sensitivity reactions may occur. One 30-year-old employee of a spice factory developed asthmatic symptoms when exposed to garlic dust. Contact dermatitis has resulted occasionally when garlic has been applied topically to skin disorders or wounds. Individuals with sensitivity should not eat garlic. The recipes below, although containing significant quantities of garlic, are known to be safe from many years of experience in Greek and other ethnic kitchens, if the garlic is eaten by non-sensitive individuals.

It must be kept in mind that cooking or heating garlic over steam may cause it to be less effective because the content of ajoene, and possibly some of the many other valuable components such as allicin, will be decreased or destroyed. You will recall that allicin is formed when garlic is cut and the precursor, alliin, is converted to allicin by the enzyme allinase, and that ajoene is found only in fresh garlic preparations.

To preserve freshness, a method used in Russia is to dip the cloves in paraffin; wrapping a clove in plastic film has also been recommended. The usual method for keeping garlic in a kitchen is to place it in a “garlic keeper” —a small, covered ceramic pot with vents. This will maintain freshness for four to six days. Many recipes demand that fresh garlic be pounded in a mortar; using a mechanical Waring-type blender will not produce the desired smooth mixtures and may result in an undesirable bitter flavor.

Traditional Garlic Preparations

Plain and Simple

The simplest preparation is to take a piece of buttered toast, put two cloves of garlic through a garlic press and spread it on the toast. Olive oil can be used instead of butter. This combination of butter or olive oil, toast and garlic is easily digested because the mixture with garlic makes a smooth emulsion. Two pieces of toast prepared in this way is the usual quantity.

Skordalia

Skordalia (Greek): This is an ancient recipe in many cookbooks and is offered as a sauce in most Greek restaurants. It can be prepared and kept in the refrigerator for several days. The vinegar is a form of preservative as well as flavor. It is an excellent way to eat garlic.

4 cloves of garlic

1/2 cup vinegar

2 cups cold mashed potatoes

1/4 cup water

1 cup select olive oil

salt and pepper

Peel the cloves of garlic and pound to a pulp in a mortar or heavy bowl. Add the mashed potatoes and continue pounding until thoroughly blended. Add the olive oil, vinegar and water, alternately, a little at a time. (The water is optional.) Continue stirring briskly for a smooth sauce, season with salt and pepper to taste and stir until well blended. Cover and store in a cool place.

Aïoli Sauce

Aïoli Sauce (French): Good for boiled fish (especially the flavorless cod), snails, boiled potatoes, boiled beef, green beans, and hard-boiled eggs.

Take a piece of stale white bread and break it up into small pieces. Add 3 tablespoons of milk or wine vinegar and let soak for 10 minutes; put the bread in a towel or cheesecloth remnant and twist it to extract the liquid. Put the bread and 4 or 5 cloves of peeled garlic into the mortar and pound until a very smooth paste results. Add 1 egg yolk and 1/8 teaspoon salt, continuing pounding until the mixture is thick. Now add, drop by drop, 1/2 to 1 cup olive oil, continuing the pounding until thick again. Add 3 to 4 tablespoonfuls of boiling water drop by drop, alternating with 2 to 3 tablespoons of lemon juice, stirring with a wire whisk. Do not add too much; the sauce should remain thick to hold its shape.

Skordalia with Aïoli Sauce

Another method of preparing Skordalia involves using Aïoli sauce. It is more difficult to prepare but is more flavorful than the traditional Greek recipe. To the thickened Aïoli sauce, add while using a wire whisk,

1/4 cup ground almonds

1/4 cup bread crumbs

3 teaspoons lemon juice

2 tablespoons chopped parsley

Saziki

Saziki (Greek): This recipe consists of nothing more than garlic put through a garlic press and mixed with yogurt and bits of cucumber. A nice dispersion forms and makes this an easy way to eat garlic. Those persons sensitive to cucumber can eliminate the cucumber.

Sauces and Spreads

Garlic base for sauces or spreads: put 4 peeled garlic clove in a large mortar and pound to a pulp; add 3/4 cup olive oil slowly while pounding, then add 1/4 cup wine vinegar slowly. A variety of spices (1/2 to 1 teaspoon) such as salt, pepper, tarragon, mustard powder, or others can be added as desired. This mixture is very similar to the basic ingredients of Skordalia, and like it, can be kept in the refrigerator as a stock but should remain good for two weeks rather than only a few days.

Note: These are recipes for eating fresh garlic. The reader is referred to the many excellent cookbooks on garlic for meals in which garlic is used only as a flavor, or in cooked form.

Grow Your Own Garlic

Garlic may be grown in your own garden, but requires patience and some luck. Bulbs may be obtained directly from supermarkets or garden supply stores. The bulbs are divided into separate cloves, planted about two inches deep and six or more inches apart, with the pointed end up. Planting is best done in the late fall, with harvest of the new bulbs in eight or nine months. Not all cloves will successfully develop into new bulbs and mold may be a problem if the ground is too moist. Mulching and fertilizing are important.

When stems appear, they should be supported or breakage may occur. Flower heads should be removed and the bulbs may be dug up when the stems become dry and brown. The harvested bulbs may be kept in a cool shaded area (basement) for up to six months, after removing the stalks and roots.

There are several types of garlic that may be grown, and some types may require specific climates and soils. Local garden supply stores can provide regional information. The most common form is "softneck garlic," which is the common white bulb. Silverskin is the favored member of this group, which also includes a stronger German Red and a milder Italian Purple. "Hardneck" garlics include Rocambole (serpent garlic), and Spanish, Yugoslavian and Russian forms. A third type, "elephant" garlic, is appearing in stores; it is very mild and has less flavor. Silverskin garlic is said to be the easiest to grow and is the most common form purchased in grocery stores. Flavors may differ depending upon local soil characteristics and this accounts for the noticeable differences in garlic from Crete, Greece, Italy and California.

Affidavits and Testimonials

In recent years, non-professional individuals, with personal interests in certain professional functions that affect their lives, have formed groups to inform each other of their experiences with the results of decisions made by professionals. When those professionals also participate in these groups, major advances in knowledge and therapeutic regimens may occur. There are many examples of such groups in the field of medicine. Individuals with experience in the use of garlic can provide the basis for formation of a similar group.

A major aim of this book, in order to collect and scientifically analyze experience with garlic, is to request the reader to fill out and send in the questionnaire at the end of this book and thereby join others who have experienced beneficial effects of garlic ingestion. That such groups can be valuable is evidenced by the success of the examples that follow.

For many years, research physicians had known that the pituitary gland of mammals contained a hormone that controlled growth. In the absence of pituitary hormones, a child becomes a type of dwarf known as "hypopituitary." For years, pituitary extracts of various species had been administered to these dwarfs without success. Then in 1959, it was discovered that only the extract from primate or human pituitary glands would cause the dwarfed child to respond and grow. It was obvious that human pituitary glands for this purpose would be in short supply.

In Columbus, Ohio, a renowned research physician had a small supply of this human extract available and treated one small boy who responded with an excellent spurt of growth. The supply was soon exhausted. The father of this child then proposed to the physician that he form a group of people to write to others with the same problems and organize them in order to visit hospitals where these pituitary glands might be collected at autopsies and sent to research physicians capable of making the extracts. By extending this effort throughout the United States, more children could be treated for longer periods of time and hopefully reach a normal adult size.

This small beginning resulted in the formation of a federally financed project to collect and process these glands (initially known as the National Pituitary Agency) and now continues as a major private research organization run by non-medical persons collecting funds for further research and advance of knowledge in all forms of growth disorders in children (The Human Growth Foundation).

Similar groups of interested parents and patients with diabetes mellitus have banded together throughout the United States and have formed the Juvenile Diabetes Foundation that meets, not only with themselves, but also with physicians. They discuss problems in management and share solutions with each other, thus educating themselves as well as their physicians about home problems. This group also has now grown into a foundation that raises money for further research in this disease.

In Chicago, 15 years ago, one of the authors was informed that his daughter had developed a curvature of the spine (scoliosis) as she began to enter adolescence. After consulting with several different specialists, the girl's father realized that each was recommending a different form of therapy. One physician proposed doing nothing about the problem, another recommended enclosing the torso in a metal cage (Milwaukee brace), and still a third recommended surgery to insert a metal bar in the spine and thus correct the curvature (Harrington bar). No information was provided as to the success ratio between these various procedures.

The father placed an advertisement in the Chicago newspapers requesting information from anyone who had faced a similar problem in the hope that knowledge of the results of each form of therapy could be evaluated. This resulted in an astonishing response of over 1,000 letters from families and patients who had experienced the same problem. As a result of organizing this group of interested individuals, there is now the Chicago chapter of The Scoliosis Association, which provides information to families and individuals facing this problem for the first time.

These three examples represent only a small portion of many such groups that include cancer patients, psychiatric patients, AIDS patients and others, all organized and achieving results that would not be accomplished without their efforts.

At the end of this book you will find a form that we encourage you to fill out and mail to the address listed. By contributing your experiences and knowledge, we hope to be able to accumulate valid statistical data that will open paths to further research and investigation into the beneficial effects of garlic. If you wish, your name will be included in the list of those who will receive copies of the final data, but no names will be published or used in any other way without permission.

As examples, we are including the following testimonial evidence from personal experience. Such evidence is always met with skepticism and disbelief by professionals. But if folklore testimonials had always been rejected as worthless and unscientific, we would not have any of the medications listed in the introduction to this book; the National Cancer Institute would not be financing the ethnobotanists listed earlier; shamanic knowledge would never receive scientific evaluation.

Casual conversations by one of the authors have revealed an astonishingly large number of people taking garlic in various quantities for a variety of reasons. We hope to enlist your cooperation in compiling and organizing the experiences of all interested persons who have examples similar to those detailed here.

Case 1.

A 50-year-old female with metastatic uterine cancer was being treated with surgery and chemotherapy. After a prolonged period of chemotherapy, her physician was pleased that there was control of the spread of cancer, but the chemotherapy had caused the usual side-effect of a very low blood count. At the suggestion of a garlic enthusiast, she began to take four cloves of garlic daily while continuing chemotherapy. Her blood count recovered toward normal and her physician attributed the recovery to a proper dosage of chemotherapy. She, therefore, stopped taking the garlic preparation. Immediately, the blood count again dropped to dangerous levels. She restarted garlic therapy and at the present time, her blood count has recovered while still following her physician's recommendations for chemotherapy. (She also reports resistance to colds and "flu" affecting other members of her immediate family.)

This case resembles the scientific study in mice reported in the medical research journal *Nutrition and Cancer*, volume 13, pages 201-207, 1990, which demonstrated that garlic afforded protection from the toxicity of chemotherapy without interfering with the tumor-reducing activity of the chemotherapeutic agent, cyclophosphamide.

Case 2.

While discussing a garlic dip at a cocktail party, two friends of the author jokingly said that "Nick would make us eat it for our health." A lady overheard the conversation and interrupted them to say "My name is Mary. I was diagnosed as having a terminal case of cancer of the lymph system. A friend of mine from India told me to eat a complete bulb of garlic every day. Since I had no other option, I peeled and crushed and ate a bulb of garlic every day. I have been doing this for five years and my disease is apparently in total remission."

This case also is supported by a study in the medical literature on the toxic effect of ajoene on cell cultures of another specific lymphoid malignancy, Burkitt's lymphoma (Goldfinger 1991). When a suitable experimental animal is found in whom lymphoid malignancies may be studied, the effect of garlic preparations should be investigated.

These are only two examples of anecdotal testimonials on the effectiveness of garlic in cancer therapy. We hope to collect many additional reports from readers who may have similar experiences that can lead to rigorous testing of a variety of malignancies in the proper scientific setting. The extensive list of references included in this book demonstrates that such testing can and must be carried out in reputable laboratories for the benefit of cancer patients.

There are additional testimonial letters from individuals convinced that garlic helps a variety of medical conditions. The following is quoted with permission.

Mr. Charles Taylor of Palmdale, California, says that he is a diabetic patient with asthma, sinus and arthritis problems and high blood pressure.

"Doctors were keeping most of my problems tolerably controlled, except the high blood pressure. They put me on different medications, which either didn't lower the blood pressure enough or caused side effects that were worse than the hypertension. While I was on these medications, I also started taking a clove of garlic in the morning, at noon and at night. My blood pressure lowered into the high-normal range, then on to normal. In a short time, people like me can forget to do the easy things like taking garlic. I did. When my blood pressure started rising again, I thought maybe it was just a coincidence. But when I started taking garlic again, I noticed the blood pressure lowered. I am now down to garlic three days a week to help keep any odor down. Also, now my blood-sugar levels seem easier to control, my legs have stopped ulcerating, I haven't had a cold in three years, the asthma is easier to live with and the arthritis doesn't hurt nearly as much as it did before." (Letter in PREVENTION magazine, June 1991, page 132.)

The evidence for garlic's effect on lowering blood sugar has been reviewed above (Jain 1973, 1975; Chang and Johnson, 1980).

Conclusions

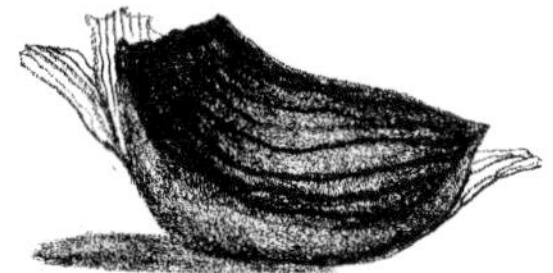

Modern research by reputable scientific investigators now supports some of the folklore beliefs about garlic. This plant product is relatively harmless and deserves further investigation. The National Cancer Institute is now supporting these investigations. Many individuals with familial cancer histories can now be identified by examining their genetic material. The only preventive techniques available to these persons are dietary, with emphasis upon added fiber and reduced fats.

The evidence reviewed here suggests that garlic may, and perhaps should, become part of a preventive regimen. A considerable amount of additional research, both basic and clinical, will be required to clarify further the mechanisms of action and a number of university laboratories have already begun these efforts. Drug companies will be coming out with costly preparations, derivatives, concentrates, etc, as they have with all other remedies from natural sources. It should be remembered, however, that the folklore history of successful therapy has been based upon the ingestion of the natural plant and its products. The research efforts, however, will be worthwhile since shamanic knowledge and folklore usage over centuries has proven the therapeutic usefulness of this remarkable plant.

About the Authors

Dr. Orville C. Green III obtained his undergraduate degree from Harvard College in 1949 and his medical degree from Northwestern University in 1954. Featured in the book, *The Best Doctors in the United States* (Wide View Books 1980), Dr. Green was included in a list of the 40 top doctors in Chicago according to a 1983 article in *Chicago Magazine*, which noted specialists physicians would go to if *they* were sick. A retired endocrinologist from Children's Memorial Hospital in Chicago, Ill., Dr. Green founded the hospital's first full-time Division of Endocrinology in 1963, which he headed until 1989. He has served as chairman of numerous committees at Children's

Memorial and at Northwestern, where he taught first as an associate and then as a full professor of pediatrics from 1963 to 1989.

Nicholas G. Polydoris is a registered professional engineer and a 1954 graduate of Northwestern University. He is president of ENM Company, a manufacturer of digital counters, which he founded in 1957. Mr. Polydoris holds a number of patents in his field. He has been a lifelong advocate of the use of fresh garlic.

References

Arora R. C. and S. Arora. "Comparative effects of clofibrate, garlic and onion on alimentary hyperlipidemia." *Atherosclerosis.* 1981; 39:447-452.

Bailey C. J. and C. Day. "Traditional plant medicines as treatment for diabetes." *Diabetes Care.* 1989; 12:553-564.

Belman S., et al. "Papilloma and carcinoma production in DMBA-initiated, onion oil-promoted mouse skin." *Nutr. Cancer.* 1990; 14:141-148.

Belman S., J. Solomon, A. Segal, E. Block, and G. Barany. "Inhibition of soybean lipoxygenase and mouse skin promotion by onion and garlic components." *J. Biochem. Toxicol.* 1989; 4:151-158.

Belman, S. "Onion and garlic oils inhibit tumor promotion." *Carcinogenesis.* 1983; 4:1063-65.

Block E., S. Ahmad, M. K. Jain, et al. "The chemistry of alkyl thiosulfate esters." 8. "Ajoene: a potent antithrombotic agent from garlic." *J. Am. Chem. Soc.* 1984; 106:8295-6.

Block E. "The chemistry of garlic and onions." *Scientific American.* 1985; 252:114-119 (March).

Bordia A., and H. C. Bansal. "Essential oil of garlic in prevention of atherosclerosis." *Lancet 2*; 1973,:1491-2.

Bordia A. "Effect of garlic on blood lipids in patients with coronary heart disease." *Amer. J. Clin. Nutr.* 1981; 34:2100-2103.

Caporaso N., S. M. Smith, and R. H. K. Eng. "Antifungal activity in human urine and serum after ingestion of garlic (Allium sativum)." *Antimicrob Agents and Chemother.* 1983; 23: 700-702.

Cavallito C. J., and J. H. Bailey. "Allicin, the antibacterial principle of Allium sativum." I. "Isolation, physical properties and antibacterial action." *J. Am. Chem. Soc.* 1944; 66:1950.

Cavallito C. J., S. S. Buck, and C. M. Suter. "Allicin, the antibacterial principle of Allium sativum." II. "Determination of the chemical structure." *J. Am. Chem. Soc.* 1944; 66:1950-51.

Chang M. J. W., and M. A. Johnson. "Effect of garlic on carbohydrate metabolism and lipid synthesis in rats." *J. Nutr.* 1980; 110:931-936.

Dausch J.G., and D. W. Nixon. "Garlic: A review of its relationship to malignant disease." *Prev. Med.* 1990; 19:346-361.

DeBoer L. W., et al. "Garlic extract prevents acute platelet thrombus formation in stenosed canine coronary arteries." *Amer. Heart. J.* 1989; 112:973-975.

DiPaolo J.A., and C. Carruthers. "The effect of allicin from garlic on tumor growth." *Cancer Res.* 1960; 20:431-434.

Fujiwara M., and T. Natata. "Induction of tumor immunity with tumor cells treated with extract of garlic (Allium sativum)." *Nature.* 1967; 216:83-84.

Fulder S. *Garlic, Nature's Original Remedy.* (Healing Arts Press, 1991).

Gargouri Y., H. Moreau, and M. V. Jain, et al. "Ajoene prevents fat digestion by human gastric lipase in vitro." *Biochem. Biophys. Acta.* 1989; 1006:137-139.

Goldfinger S. E. "Garlic. Good for what ails you?" *Harvard Health Letter*, volume 16, number 10, August 1991.

Goleman D. "Shamans and their longtime lore may vanish with the forests." *The New York Times*. June 11, 1991, pages B1, B9.

Jain R. C., and C. R. Vyas. "Garlic in alloxan-induced diabetic rabbits." *Am. J. Clin. Nutr.* 1975; 28:684-685.

Jain R. C., C. R. Vyas, and O. P. Mahatma. "Hypoglycemic action of onion and garlic." *Lancet*. 1973; 2:1491.

Kandil O. M., T. H. Abdullah, and A. Elkadi. "Garlic and the immune system in humans. Its effect on natural killer cells of the immune system." *Fed. Proc.* 1987; 46:441 (Abstract #73).

Lau, B., et al. "Allium Sativum (Garlic) and atherosclerosis; a review." *Nutr. Res.* 1983; 3:119-128.

Martin D. S. "Experts press garlic's health benefits." *Science and Health.* September 2, 1990, p 39.

Meng C-L., and K. W. Shyu. "Inhibition of experimental carcinogenesis by painting with garlic extract." *Nutr. Cancer*. 1990; 14:207-217.

Perchellet J. P., E. M. Perchellet, and S. Belman. "Inhibition of DMBA-induced mouse skin tumorigenesis by garlic oil and inhibition of two tumor-promotion stages by garlic and onion oils." *Nutr. Cancer*. 1990; 14:183-193.

Perchellet J. P., E. M. Perchellet, N. L. Abney, J. A. Zirnstein, and S. Belman. "Effects of garlic and onion oils on glutathione peroxidase activity, the ratio of reduced/oxidized glutathione and ornithine decarboxylase induction in isolated mouse epidermal cells treated with tumor promotors." *Cancer Biochem. Biophys.* 1986; 8:299-312.

Shyu K. W., and C.L. Meng "The inhibitory effect of four chemicals on experimental carcinogenesis." *J. Med. Sci.* 1986; 6:221-230.

Stoll A., and E. Seedback. "Chemical investigation of alliin, the specific principle of garlic." *Adv. Enzymol.* 1951; 11:377-400.

Wattenberg L. W., V. L. Sparnins, and G. Barany. "Inhibition of N-nitrosodimethylamine carcinogenesis in mice by naturally occurring organosulfur compounds and monoterperns." *Cancer Res.* 1989; 49:2689-2692.

Weisberger A. S., and J. Pensky. "Tumor inhibiting effects derived from an active principle of garlic (Allium sativum)." *Science.* 1957; 126:1112-1114.

Weisberger A. S., and J. Pensky. "Tumor inhibition by a sulfhydryl-blocking agent related to an active principle of garlic (Allium sativum)." *Cancer Res.* 1958; 18:1301-1308.

Yang C.S., J.Y. Hong, and Z.Y. Wang. "Garlic chemicals (including diallyl sulfide) prevented liver damage in rats given acetaminophen in toxic doses; also prevented growth of lung tumors induced by tobacco smoke." *Amer. Chem. Society Meeting.* August 1992.

You W-C., W. J. Blot, Y-S. Chang, A. Ershow, and Z. T. Yang, et al. "Allium vegetables and reduced risk of stomach cancer." *J. Natl. Cancer Inst.* 1989; 81:162-164.

Appendix

Aspirin: from willow bark (Salix alba). Known to ancient shamans. Multiple effects when eaten: (1) Analgesic, (2) Antipyretic, (3) Anti-inflammatory, (4) Uricosuric (causes excretion of uric acid and thereby treats gout), (5) Anti-coagulation effect, useful in prevention of heart attacks. Toxicity occurs when blood levels exceed 45 mg/dl in the blood, variable in individuals.

Atropine: from Atropa belladonna, the "deadly nightshade" plant; also from Datura stramonium, the Jimson weed. This drug is one of a family known as the belladonna drugs, with "antimuscarinic" actions, variable according to dose. These actions affect mental function, pupil of eye (dilates), dry most bodily secretions, alter heart rate, inhibit urination. Nonaddictive.

Belladonna: see atropine.

Cathartics: castor oil from seeds of Ricinus communis, senna from dried leaves of Cassia acutifolia, cascara sagrada (sacred bark) from buckthorn tree.

Cocaine: from Erythroxylon coca tree leaves that grow in Peru and Bolivia. Blocks nerve conduction when applied locally (anesthetic); affects mental function; increases body temperature; affects heart rate; constricts eye pupils. Severe toxicity with doses as low as 20 mg; fatal at about 1.2 grams. Addictive. Chemical alterations of basic structure provide local anesthetics of "-caine" types (Lidocaine, Benzocaine, Procaine - marketed as Novocaine, and many others). Procaine and all derivatives are the result of a chemical laboratory search for modifications of cocaine, not only for anesthetic uses but also for the side effects on heart arryhthmias. An entire therapeutic regimen for heart arrythmias has emerged from this search, with basic concepts of cardiac receptors of alpha and beta types.

Colchicine: from Colchicum autumnale, a plant also known as autumn crocus or meadow saffron. (Crocus was a mythological Greek youth who was transformed into a saffron plant.) Used for treatment of gout as far back as 1763. Benjamin Franklin is said to have brought it from France to America to treat himself.

Curare: originally a crude mixture of plant extracts kept secret for centuries by tribal witch doctors of the Amazon and Orinoco river areas. Asiatic, African and Australian shamans also make similar mixtures. Some of these have never been clarified. The botanical genus Erythrina (shrubs and trees) grows around the world in tropical areas and the seeds are used with other plant mixtures by these shamans. Research continues and some synthetic compounds (Pancuronium, Tubocurarine, etc.) have become useful for muscular paralysis during surgery but the shamanic secret mixtures remain unknown.

Digitalis: the best known cardiac glycoside; from the foxglove plant, Digitalis purpurea. Also from Digitalis lanata. Dried leaves are the form of therapy for heart failure and certain arrhythmias. Used in Wales as far back as 1250.

Digitoxin: from the seeds of Digitalis plant. More potent than digitalis leaf.

Digoxin: cardiac glycoside from leaves of Digitalis lanata.

Ergot: from a fungus that grows on grains, especially rye. Has been known for over 2,000 years as causing abortions, accelerated delivery or premature delivery of babies; causes blood vessel constriction and subsequent gangrene; contaminated rye caused St. Anthony's Fire, a painful disease of the extremities occurring in epidemics in the Middle Ages. Ancient Greeks and Romans would not eat rye and possibly knew of these effects. Derivatives (ergotamine) are useful today for migraine headache and induction of uterine contractions.

Laxatives: bran; agar from seaweed; tragacanth from Astragallis gummifer; gum arabic from Acacia senegal.

Opiates: opium comes from the juice of poppy capsules and has been known for over 4,000 years (Sumerians). Laudanum, an opium mixture, was introduced by Paracelsus in the early 16th century. Used for dysentery; constipating; addictive. Morphine isolated from opium in 1803 (named after the Greek god Morpheus); codeine isolated in 1832; papaverine in 1848. In spite of continuing laboratory research, no nonaddictive derivatives have been developed. Multiple organ system effects: relieves pain, sedates, causes constipation, suppresses cough, relieves the shortness of breath of heart failure. Oliver Wendell Holmes (M.D.) commented that there were only two useful medical agents in his day: opium (morphine) and digitalis leaf.

Ouabaine: a cardiac glycoside (see digitalis) from the seeds of the plant, Strophanthus gratus.

Picrotoxin: from the seeds of the shrub Anamirta cocculus, from the East Indies. A stimulant to the central nervous system producing convulsive seizures; once used to treat overdose poisoning by drugs depressing mental function; no longer used clinically but has many research laboratory uses.

Psoralens: from a variety of plants; known to ancient Egyptians as a weed; also in buttercups, figs, limes, and parsnips. When eaten and followed by sun exposure, the skin darkens. Now being used experimentally in making blood supplies safer by killing viruses (hepatitis, AIDS) and bacteria, in conjunction with irradiation of the blood supply with ultraviolet light.

Quinidine: from cinchona bark; was found to be of use in cardiac arrhythmias because of an observation in 1749 that patients being treated with quinine, and who also had heart arrythmias, were cured of both. Also depresses skeletal muscle. Quinidine and quinine are both found in the same tree bark. (A synthetic derivative of cocaine, procaineamide, is now the drug of choice over quinidine for heart arrythmias.)

Quinine: first written about in 1633 by an Augustinian monk named Calancha, in Lima, Peru. From cinchona tree bark. Became famous as an antimalarial drug but it affects many organ systems, probably all: local anesthetic, central nervous system (analgesia), lowers fevers, stimulates vomiting, causes ringing in the ears and vertigo, has cardiovascular effects, causes uterine contractions and abortions, affects skeletal muscle by relieving cramps, affects gastrointestinal tract. But therapeutic usage is limited to the antimalarial effect and the relief of nocturnal leg cramps. Very toxic in large doses; 8 grams is fatal. Toxicity is termed "cinchonism."

Reserpine: from the shrub Rauwolfia serpentina. Recorded in ancient Hindu writings and used for many years in India for insanity, sleeplessness, and high blood pressure. Induces a state of calm indifference to uncomfortable environmental stimuli and is said to have been chewed by Gandhi while negotiating India's freedom from Britain. Inhibits cyclic menstruation and fertility. Now has been replaced in psychiatry by more potent antipsychotic drugs but still has occasional uses.

Scopolamine: also called hyoscine; from the shrub Hyoscyamus niger (henbane); also from Scopolia carniolica. Another antimuscarinic drug (see atropine) but used more for causing amnesia, drowsiness, dreamless sleep; useful as a preanesthetic.

Squill: an extract of the "sea onion," Urginia maritima. Acts like other cardiac glycosides (see digitalis). Known to the ancient Egyptians and Romans. No longer an official medical drug because of replacement by modern synthetics.

Strychnine: a toxic alkaloid present in the seeds of the tree, Strychnos nux vomica. Used as a rat poison now; no legitimate medical use.

Taxol: extract from the bark of the yew tree, effective in several cancers, especially ovarian cancer. Now the subject of a fight with environmentalists who fear destruction of all yew trees before this drug can be synthesized and made available in quantity. A synthetic derivative, taxotere (RP56976) is under research study at the National Cancer Institute.

Vinblastine, Vincristine: "Vinca alkaloids" - anticancer drugs from the periwinkle plant; used successfully in a variety of cancers, including leukemia.

Vitamins: Vitamin B complex and Nicotinic Acid from rice polishings; Vitamin C from fruits and vegetables; Vitamin A from yellow vegetables; Vitamin K from alfalfa, chloroplasts of many leaves and vegetable oils; Vitamin E from wheat germ oil. Vitamin supplementation is not necessary when a well rounded diet is consumed.

For additional information on these drugs, their medical use, indications, dosage, and side effects, the interested reader is referred to the standard textbook, The *Pharmacological Basis of Therapeutics* by L. S. Goodman and Alfred Gilman, Macmillan Publishing Company, New York. There are additional plant derivatives from folklore medicine being researched at Harvard University, the University of California in San Francisco, and Upjohn Laboratories: Lithospermeum ruterale (a plant with contraceptive activity from folklore of American Indians), and gossypol, a component of cottonseed oil, which is a folklore contraceptive of Chinese women. Gossypol has been shown to be destructive to the structure of sperm.

Glossary

Amino acids, Essential (8): Isoleucine, Leucine, Lysine, Methionine, Phenylalanine, Threonine, Tryptophane, Valine. (Methionine, $C_5H_{11}NO_2S$, is the only one containing sulfur.)

Amino acids, Nonessential (12): Alanine, Arginine, Aspartic acid, Citrulline, Cystine, Glutamic acid, Glycine, Histidine, Hydroxyproline, Proline, Serine, Tyrosine. Of the 12 nonessential amino acids, only cystine, ($C_6H_{12}N_2O_4S_2$), contains sulfur.

Ajoene: Chemical structure: $CH_2=CH-CH_2-S(O)CH_2-CH=CH-S-S-CH_2CH=CH_2$.

Allicin: Diallyl disulfide-oxide: Chemical structure: $CH_2=CH-CH_2-S(O)-S-CH_2-CH=CH_2$.

Allyl: from Allium, generic name for some members of the Lily family. Wertheim used this term to signify a chemical structure that unites two carbon atoms by a double bond, with the configuration $CH_2=CH-CH_2-$.

Antihelminthic: a medication that kills worms, usually applied to worms infesting the body.

Antimicrobial: a drug that kills or suppresses microbes.

Antimuscarinic: drugs that oppose the "muscarinic" actions of acetylcholine; antimuscarinic actions are similar to those of the drug atropine, interfering with certain nerve and muscle actions.

Antithrombotic: a drug that prevents blood clotting.

Atherosclerosis: aging and stiffening of arteries associated with deposits or plaques of fats and cholesterol.

Carbon atoms separated by a double bond: refers to a form of bonding of carbon atoms, which is "unsaturated" and is drawn as -C=C-.

Carcinogen: a compound that is suspected to cause cancer.

Chemotherapy: a regimen of treatment involving drugs that will suppress or eradicate cancer cells.

Cyclophosphamide: one of the chemotherapeutic drugs.

Diallyl disulfide: in garlic; allylic compound with two sulfur atoms. Chemical structure: CH2=CH-CH2-S-S-CH2-CH=CH2.

Diallyl disulfide-oxide (allicin): chemical structure: CH2=CH-CH2-S(O)-S-CH2-CH=CH2.

Diallyl tetrasulfide: in garlic; allylic compound with four sulfur atoms.

Diallyl trisulfide: in garlic; allylic compound with three sulfur atoms.

Double bond: see carbon atom.

Endorphins: the word is a combination of "endogenous" and "morphine;" chemicals found in the pituitary gland, which are released and act in the brain like exogenous morphine acts.

Enkephalin: a specific type of endorphin with morphine-like activity.

Enzyme: a protein acting on substrates to perform a reaction.

Ethnobotany: the study of plants used in ethnic societies for purposes other than food (medical uses, etc.).

Exogenous: external to the body.

Hypoglycemia: a blood sugar level below the normal level; usually considered to be below 40 mg per 100 ml blood.

Margin of safety: the safe dosage range of a drug between the dose needed for therapeutic effect and the quantity needed to reach a toxic effect. The wider the range (margin), the safer the drug.

Milligram (mg): one onethousandth of a gram of weight.

Milliliter (ml): one onethousandth of a liter of liquid.

Mutation: a change in the genetic material of any form of life. May be advantageous or harmful with respect to natural selection. Mutations are required for evolution to occur.

Natural selection: Charles Darwin's explanation for "the survival of the fittest" whereby the most adaptable species will survive the rigors of environmental or other threats; also applied to evolutionary development of the most successful internal biological mechanisms.

Nitrosamines: certain chemicals, usually produced by charring food, or may be found in preserved foods or burned foods, and which have been shown to be carcinogenic.

Pituitary gland: a small gland situated in the center of the head; also called the "master gland" because its secretions control many other glands besides secreting the hormone that controls childhood growth - Growth Hormone.

Platelets, platelet aggregation: platelets are small cellular elements in the blood stream that, under certain conditions, clump together (aggregate) and begin clot formation.

Potency: when applied to drugs, is an indication of therapeutic or toxic effect per milligram or per milliliter.

Receptor: in biology, applied to the specific proteins that will attract and bind another substance, either within cells or extracellular.

Research, basic: applied to that type of research that is carried out to clarify fundamental theories and hypotheses; usually work done at a laboratory bench or in specially designed environments.

Research, clinical: utilizing human subjects to test products or techniques usually resulting from basic research.

Shaman: refers to one who acts as both priest and medicine man, usually in primitive societies.

Substrate: in chemistry, the substance acted upon by an enzyme or chemical reaction, thereby producing a new substance.

Vermifuge: a product that will rid the body of parasitic worms. An antihelminthic.

QUESTIONNAIRE

Name: ____

Age: ______

Health Disorder: ______________________________________

(If no health disorder, skip to question 5)

hysician's recommended treatment: ______________________________

____

____

hat is your physician's attitude on your use of garlic? ____________________

____

____

Recommends garlic:

☐ Yes ☐ No ☐ Objects, but permits it

☐ Doesn't care ☐ Forbids it

f forbidden, why? ______________________________________

____

Iow do you take garlic?

☐ Entire clove ☐ Cooked ☐ Kyolic

☐ Pressed pulp ☐ Pills ☐ Powder

Other: ____

Quantity you take: ______________________________________

Daily? Yes___ No___ If not daily, how often? ______________________

Iow long have you taken this amount of garlic? ______________________

Do you think garlic has been helpful? Yes___ No ___

f yes, why? ____

f you stopped taking garlic, why did you stop? ______________________

____

f you are continuing, has the odor persisted? ______________________

Iave there been other problems? ________________________________

Optional:

ddress: ____

treet, State, Zip: ______________________________________

lease give your address if you wish a final report of this survey. No names of individuals will be ublished and all responses will be kept confidential. Please use other side for additional omments or requests.

Mail QUESTIONNAIRE back to : P.O. Box 321, Kenilworth, IL 60043